CAREER ANCHORS

CAREER ANCHORS:
Discovering Your Real Values

Revised Edition

Edgar H. Schein, Ph.D.

Alfred P. Sloan School of Management
Massachusetts Institute of Technology

San Francisco

Copyright © 1993 by Jossey-Bass/Pfeiffer

ISBN: 0-89384-210-9 (U.S.: pbk)
Library of Congress Catalog Card Number 92-40385

Library of Congress Cataloging-in-Publication Data

Schein, Edgar H.

    Career anchors: discovering your real values/Edgar H. Schein.—Rev. ed.
       p.   cm.
    ISBN 0-89384-210-9 (U.S.: pbk)
    1. Vocational guidance.   I. Title.
HF5381.S345   1993
331.7'02—dc20

Printed in the United States of America

Published by

Jossey-Bass
Pfeiffer

350 Sansome Street, 5th Floor
San Francisco, California 94104-1342
(415) 433-1740; Fax (415) 433-0499
(800) 274-4434; Fax (800) 569-0443

Visit our website at: http://www.pfeiffer.com

Outside of the United States, Pfeiffer products can be purchased from the following Simon & Schuster International Offices:

Prentice Hall
Campus 400
Maylands Avenue
Hemel Hempstead
Hertfordshire HP2 7EZ
United Kingdom
44(0) 1442 881891; Fax 44(0) 1442 882074

Prentice Hall Professional
Locked Bag 507
Frenchs Forest PO NSW 2086
Australia
61 2 9454 2200; Fax 61 2 9453 0089

Simon & Schuster (Asia) Pte Ltd
317 Alexandra Road
#04–01 IKEA Building
Singapore 159965
Asia
65 476 4688; Fax 65 378 0370

Prentice Hall/Pfeiffer
P.O. Box 1636
Randburg 2125
South Africa
27 11 781 0780; Fax 27 11 781 0781

Printing 10 9 8

Contents

Acknowledgments

The original research on which this booklet is based was conducted with the support of the Office of Naval Research[1] and the Massachusetts Institute of Technology Sloan School of Management. The work was originally reported in E.H. Schein, *Career Dynamics: Matching Individual and Organizational Needs* (Reading, MA: Addison-Wesley, 1978) and in E.H. Schein, "Individuals and Careers," in J. Lorsch (Ed.), *Handbook of Organizational Behavior* (Englewood Cliffs, NJ: Prentice-Hall, 1985).

An earlier version of this instrument was developed in 1980 by E.H. Schein and Howard Denmark of the CIBA-Geigy Corporation for use within that company. It was revised in 1981 with support from the International Management Institute, Geneva, Switzerland, and was first published by University Associates (now Pfeiffer & Company) in 1985.

The original version of the Career Orientation Inventory was based on work carried out by E.H. Schein and T.J. DeLong of Brigham Young University, Provo, Utah, from 1979 through 1982.

1

Introduction

This book is designed to help you to identify your career anchor and to think about how your values relate to your career choices. When you know your career anchor, you empower yourself to confront career choices and decisions in a manner consistent with what you truly value and how you really see yourself.

Your career anchor is a combination of perceived areas of competence, motives, and values that you would not give up; it represents your real self. Without knowledge of your anchor, you might be tempted by outside incentives into situations or jobs that subsequently are not satisfactory because you feel that "this is not really me." The questionnaire and interview suggested in this book are intended to help you to avoid such situations.

Regardless of your present job or career, your future decisions will be easier and more valid if you have a clear understanding of your own orientation toward work, your motives, your values, and your self-perceived talents. Such understanding will be enhanced by the activities suggested in this book.

The activities suggested are not tests, nor will they reveal hidden talents. Rather they represent a systematic way to explore your own past activities and future aspirations in order to get a clearer picture of yourself and the qualities in you that you may not have thought much about or may take for granted.

Research on career anchors has shown that most people see themselves in terms of the eight categories that will be described in the following sections. However, the important part of this exercise is the actual answering of the orientation questionnaire and participation in the mutual interview, because the categories do not mean anything outside the context of your own past history and future aspirations. It is the thinking and talking about career and life events that gradually give you a more explicit understanding of your own priorities and values.

Most people who have done the interview have enjoyed it. This may be the first time you have spent several hours talking about yourself and your career with a willing and interested listener.

How to Use This Book

This book contains several sections, including a general definition of the nature of career anchors, a discussion of career development, and detailed descriptions of the eight career anchor types. To go through the activities recommended takes three to four hours, but they need not be done all at one time. The instructions below are designed to be completely self-explanatory and will guide you through the process step by step.

It is recommended that you begin by filling in the Career Orientations Inventory that begins on page 6. Complete the scoring sheet, but do not concern yourself with your scores or with the labeling of the columns. Go on to read the next section that explains career development and the meaning of the career anchor categories that have been identified in prior research.

The most important part of the analysis is the interview with a partner. Unless you talk out your own career history with someone else, you will not really confront the pattern of talents, motives, and values that your career decisions and aspirations reflect.

Interviewing someone else about his or her career also is helpful. You and your partner can plan to interview each other, but not necessarily at the same session. Each interview typically lasts from one to two hours. Ideally, your partner also should have a copy of the *Career Anchors* book if you are both doing the exercise.

How to Select a Partner

Choose a partner with whom you will feel free to share the events of your career so far, as well as your future aspirations. For this reason, it is best to avoid a superior or subordinate or a peer with whom you may be in competition. Your partner does not have to be the same age you are or be in the same type of work. Many people report that a spouse or a close friend makes a good partner.

Your partner does not have to have any training as an interviewer; all of the questions to be asked are provided in this book. All that is needed is some interest and willingness to discuss your career with you.

2

Career Orientations Inventory

The purpose of this questionnaire is to stimulate your thoughts about your own areas of competence, your motives, and your values. This questionnaire alone will not reveal your career anchor because it is too easy to bias your answers. However, it will activate your thinking and prepare you for the discussion with your partner.

Try to answer the questions as honestly as you can and work quickly. Avoid extreme ratings except in situations in which you clearly have strong feelings in one direction or the other.

How to Rate the Items

For each of the next forty items, rate how true that item is for you in general by assigning a number from 1 to 6. The higher the number, the more that item is true for you. For example, if the item says "I dream of being the president of a company," you would rate that as follows:

"1" if the statement is never true for you

"2" or "3" if the statement is occasionally true for you

"4" or "5" if the statement is often true for you

"6" if the statement is always true for you

Career Orientations Inventory

Use the following scale to rate how true each of the items is for you and write the number in the blank.

Never True for Me	Occasionally True for Me		Often True for Me		Always True for Me
1	2	3	4	5	6

___ 1. I dream of being so good at what I do that my expert advice will be sought continually.

___ 2. I am most fulfilled in my work when I have been able to integrate and manage the efforts of others.

___ 3. I dream of having a career that will allow me the freedom to do a job my own way and on my own schedule.

___ 4. Security and stability are more important to me than freedom and autonomy.

___ 5. I am always looking for ideas that would permit me to start my own enterprise.

___ 6. I will feel successful in my career only if I have a feeling of having made a real contribution to the welfare of society.

___ 7. I dream of a career in which I can solve problems or win in situations that are extremely challenging.

___ 8. I would rather leave my organization than be put into a job that would compromise my ability to pursue personal and family concerns.

___ 9. I will feel successful in my career only if I can develop my technical or functional skills to a very high level of competence.

Never True for Me	Occasionally True for Me		Often True for Me		Always True for Me
1	2	3	4	5	6

___10. I dream of being in charge of a complex organization and of making decisions that affect many people.

___11. I am most fulfilled in my work when I am completely free to define my own tasks, schedules, and procedures.

___12. I would rather leave my organization altogether than accept an assignment that would jeopardize my security in that organization.

___13. Building my own business is more important to me than achieving a high-level managerial position in someone else's organization.

___14. I am most fulfilled in my career when I have been able to use my talents in the service of others.

___15. I will feel successful in my career only if I face and overcome very difficult challenges.

___16. I dream of a career that will permit me to integrate my personal, family, and work needs.

___17. Becoming a senior functional manager in my area of expertise is more attractive to me than becoming a general manager.

___18. I will feel successful in my career only if I become a general manager in some organization.

___19. I will feel successful in my career only if I achieve complete autonomy and freedom.

___20. I seek jobs in organizations that will give me a sense of security and stability.

Never True for Me	Occasionally True for Me		Often True for Me		Always True for Me
1	2	3	4	5	6

___21. I am most fulfilled in my career when I have been able to build something that is entirely the result of my own ideas and efforts.

___22. Using my skills to make the world a better place in which to live and work is more important to me than achieving a high-level managerial position.

___23. I have been most fulfilled in my career when I have solved seemingly unsolvable problems or won out over seemingly impossible odds.

___24. I feel successful in life only if I have been able to balance my personal, family, and career requirements.

___25. I would rather leave my organization than accept a rotational assignment that would take me out of my area of expertise.

___26. Becoming a general manager is more attractive to me than becoming a senior functional manager in my current area of expertise.

___27. The chance to do a job my own way, free of rules and constraints, is more important to me than security.

___28. I am most fulfilled in my work when I feel that I have complete financial and employment security.

___29. I will feel successful in my career only if I have succeeded in creating or building something that is entirely my own product or idea.

___30. I dream of having a career that makes a real contribution to humanity and society.

Never	Occasionally		Often		Always
True	True		True		True
for Me	for Me		for Me		for Me
1	2	3	4	5	6

___31. I seek out work opportunities that strongly challenge my problem-solving and/or competitive skills.

___32. Balancing the demands of my personal and professional lives is more important to me than achieving a high-level managerial position.

___33. I am most fulfilled in my work when I have been able to use my special skills and talents.

___34. I would rather leave my organization than accept a job that would take me away from the general managerial path.

___35. I would rather leave my organization than accept a job that would reduce my autonomy and freedom.

___36. I dream of having a career that will allow me to feel a sense of security and stability.

___37. I dream of starting up and building my own business.

___38. I would rather leave my organization than accept an assignment that would undermine my ability to be of service to others.

___39. Working on problems that are almost unsolvable is more important to me than achieving a high-level managerial position.

___40. I have always sought out work opportunities that would minimize interference with my personal or family concerns.

Look over your answers and locate the items that you rated highest. Pick out the THREE items that seem most true for you and give *each* of those items an additional FOUR (4) points. Score your questionnaire. The scales will not have real meaning for you until you have read the text in the next sections.

Scoring Instructions

Transfer the numbers from your rating sheets onto the scoring sheet. After you have transferred all of the numbers, add up the columns and divide by five (the number of items) to get your average score for each of the eight career anchor dimensions. Do not forget to add the extra four points for *each* of your three key items before you total and average your scores.

The resulting average is your self-assessment of how true the items in that scale are for you. Explanations of the columns will be provided later in this book.

Scoring Sheet

	TF	GM	AU	SE	EC	SV	CH	LS
	1 __	2 __	3 __	4 __	5 __	6 __	7 __	8 __
	9 __	10 __	11 __	12 __	13 __	14 __	15 __	16 __
	17 __	18 __	19 __	20 __	21 __	22 __	23 __	24 __
	25 __	26 __	27 __	28 __	29 __	30 __	31 __	32 __
	33 __	34 __	35 __	36 __	37 __	38 __	39 __	40 __
TOTAL:	__	__	__	__	__	__	__	__
	÷5	÷5	÷5	÷5	÷5	÷5	÷5	÷5
Average:	__	__	__	__	__	__	__	__

3

Career Development

The word *career* is used in many different ways and has many connotations. Sometimes "having a career" is used to apply only to someone who has a profession or whose occupational life is well-structured and involves steady advancement. In the context of career anchors, *career* includes how any individual's work life develops over time and how it is perceived by that person.

One might consider this to be the "internal career," to distinguish it from what others might view that person's work life to be. Everyone has some kind of picture of his or her work life and role in that life. It is this internal picture that will be explored here in some detail in discussing the concept of career anchors.

To distinguish "internal career" from other uses of the word, we will use "external career" to refer to the actual steps that are required by an occupation or an organization for progress through that occupation. A physician must complete medical school, internship, residency, specialty board examinations, and so on. In some organizations a general manager has to go through several business functions, have experience in supervising people, take on a functional management job, rotate through the international division, and serve on the corporate staff before being given a true generalist job as a division general manager. Some organizations talk of career paths, which define the necessary—or at least desirable—steps for the career occupant to take along the way to some goal job.

What follows is an outline of the major stages of the external career and some of the dimensions along which one can measure career movement or progress. Next is a description of the evolution of the internal career and the concept of career anchor, the self-image that a person develops around his or her career which comes to be a guide as well as a constraint on career decisions. The implications of the career anchor concept for human resource management will be explored from the individual career occupant's point of view as well as from the point of view of the supervisor.

Major Stages of the Career[2]

From the individual's point of view, a career consists of several meaningful units or stages that are recognized both by the person and by society, although the length of time associated with each unit or stage varies immensely according to the occupation and the individual within it. These ten stages are described in the sections that follow and are depicted in Figure 1.

Stage 1: Growth, fantasy, and exploration. In this period, usually associated with childhood and early adolescence, an occupation is a mere thought, and a career has little meaning except in terms of occupational stereotypes and a general goal of "success." The person at this stage prepares to enter the necessary training or educational process for whatever occupation is tentatively chosen.

Stage 2: Education and training. Depending on the occupation, this process can be very elaborate or very minimal, lasting anywhere from a few months to twenty or more years. There are many choice points during this stage as occupational goals are clarified and changed. In some occupations (such as medicine), the external career stages require early decision making to ensure that all of the

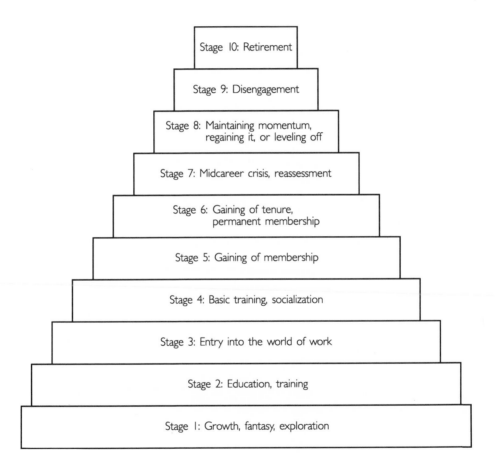

Figure I. Major Stages of the Career

prerequisites for later entry are achieved during the period of education.

Stage 3: Entry into the world of work. For most people, regardless of their levels of preparation, this is a time of major adjustment as they learn about the realities of work and their own reactions. In particular, the educational process rarely prepares people for the seemingly irrational and political side of organizational life or for the fact that much of the work in every occupation involves not only logic and reason but also working with people and their feelings. Major personal learning begins at this point, and an occupational self-concept begins to evolve as the career incumbent begins to test his or her own talents, motives, and values in the crucible of real work.

Stage 4: Basic training and socialization. The length and the intensity of this period differ by occupation, organization, complexity of the work, the organization's assumptions about the importance of teaching elements of the culture to the new members, and the degree of responsibility that society assigns to the occupation. The more responsible the occupation, the longer and more intense the socialization period. This stage is a major source of personal learning because the organization now begins to make demands to which the individual must respond. The career occupant is faced with real choices about whether or not to remain in the occupation and/or the organization, depending on how he or she responds to the socialization process.

Stage 5: Gaining of membership. At some point an individual recognizes through formal rituals or the kinds of assignments received that he or she has passed beyond the trainee stage and has been accepted as a full contributor. At this stage a meaningful self-image as a member of the occupation or organization begins to emerge. Motives and values begin to be clarified through seeing one's responses to different challenging situations in which choices must be made. One begins to have a better sense of one's talents, strengths, and weaknesses.

Stage 6: Gaining of tenure and permanent membership. Within the first five to ten years of a career, most organizations and occupations make a tenure decision that tells the individual whether or not he or she can count on a long-term future in the organization. Tenure is formally or symbolically granted with the proviso that tenure exists only so long as a job exists. In some occupations (such as university teaching), the tenure process forces the organization either to grant formal tenure or to ask the person to leave. In most organizations the process is not that formalized but operates, nevertheless, through norms pertaining to seniority or layoffs.

Stage 7: Midcareer crisis and reassessment. Although it is not clear whether this is a crisis or even a stage, there is mounting evidence that most people go through some kind of reassessment of themselves when they are well into their careers, asking themselves questions about their initial choices ("Have I entered the right career?"), about their levels of attainment ("Have I accomplished all I hoped to accomplish?" or "What have I accomplished and was it worth the sacrifices?"), and about their futures ("Should I continue or make a change?" or "What do I want to do with the rest of my life, and how does my work fit into it?"). Such reassessment can be traumatic, but many people find it to be normal and relatively painless, often leading to a rediscovery or reaffirmation of goals that have been present but not salient. When people make such goals more prominent, they sometimes appear to be making major career changes. However, such changes rarely are experienced as big events by the career occupant. Rather, they tend to be experienced as "Finally I am doing more of what I really want to do with my life!"

Stage 8: Maintaining momentum, regaining it, or leveling off. The insights that result from reassessment result in decisions about how the remainder of one's career will be pursued. Each person at this stage develops a personal solution that will guide his or her next steps. For some this is a determination to climb the ladder as far as possible; for some it is a redefining of the areas of work they wish to pursue; and for many it involves a complex assessment of how to balance the demands of work, family, and personal concerns. Those whose talents force them to level off may face a difficult psychological adjustment. However, for many people at this stage, leveling off is a choice based on the realization that one's talents, motives, and values do not require one to aspire any further.

Stage 9: Disengagement. Inevitably a person slows down, becomes less involved, begins to think about retirement, and prepares for that stage. However, some people deal with potential retirement by aggressively denying its reality, by continuing business as usual, and by actively avoiding the attempts of others to get them involved in such preparation.

Stage 10: Retirement. Whether or not the individual has prepared for it, inevitably the organization or occupation no longer makes a meaningful role available, and the individual must adjust. What happens to occupational self-image at this time varies greatly from person to person. Some people retire early because the occupation encourages it (for example, the military or professional sports) or because they want to and are able to enter different kinds of occupations early enough in life to develop second careers. For others, retirement is traumatic, resulting in loss of physical or psychological health, sometimes to the point of premature death.

These stages provide a kind of internal timetable for every person. However, the stages can be long or short, can repeat themselves if the person moves from one career to another, and are not related in any necessary fashion to age. Within a given occupation, stage may correlate with age, but the relationship between stages and age for a doctor, a clerk, a manager, a storekeeper, an engineer, and a consultant all differ.

Career Movement, Progress, or Success

The standards by which an individual measures his or her own success may be quite different from those used by another person or by society at large. In fact, the subjective definition of success largely reflects one's career anchor or internal career definition. All progress can be measured along three basic dimensions, which correspond to the

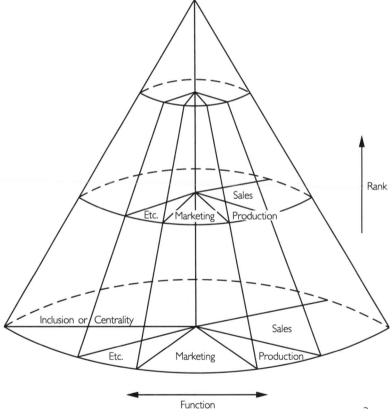

Figure 2. A Three-Dimensional Model of an Organization[3]

movement within an organization or occupation. These dimensions are shown in Figure 2 as an organizational cone.

Cross-Functional Horizontal Movement: Growth in Abilities and Skills

As people move into careers, they change in terms of what they are able to do and how well they are able to do it. Such development may be the result of their own efforts or may be correlated with specified training or development, opportunities provided by the employer or profession. This kind of movement corresponds to cross-functional rotation or formal training and development, and it results in changes in the work an individual does. It also reflects the growing tendency for workers to trade jobs and to be certified in a number of different skills. Pay systems acknowledge this form of organizational movement in the trend to pay workers for the number of skills they use.

Cross-Level Hierarchical Movement: Up the Ladder

Every occupation or organization maintains some hierarchy or system of ranks and titles by which a career occupant can judge his or her progress. Success then is a function of attaining or surpassing the level to which a person aspires.

Again, the assessments of others may differ from those of the individual. One entrepreneur who made two-million dollars felt like a failure because his friends all owned 300-million-dollar companies. Another person who leveled off in middle management felt very successful because he went so far beyond the level that his father had attained.

Without knowing a person's aspiration level, one cannot judge that person's subjective feelings of success. Level of aspiration is influenced by how society defines success, resulting in some correlation between aspirations and external criteria. Yet the external criteria will be those relevant within a given occupation, not just those of society as a whole. Money may be a general indicator of success in the United States, but engineers may judge the number of patents to be more important. For professors, the prestige of the university and fame among colleagues may matter more than money. Managers often put more value on the sizes of the budgets they control than on their actual salaries. To understand an individual's criteria for success, one must understand what that individual views as his or her reference group.

Movement In: Attaining Influence and Power

One important criterion used to judge success is the extent to which an individual feels that he or she has penetrated the inner circle of an organization or occupation. Such penetration often is correlated with hierarchical movement, but it may be achieved independently. For example, an employee who has leveled off, but who is consulted by more senior, high-ranking people by virtue of his or her experience, seniority, or personality, still influences policy. Many technical people in organizations enjoy this kind of influence. Often, secretaries have power and influence far beyond their formal positions, resulting from informal contacts that have been built over the years.

Because such movement is invisible, judging its impact is difficult without talking to the individual. A person may feel very successful because of the sense of being in the inner circle and having influence; unless others ask about this, they may misjudge that person's sense of success. Sometimes one even encounters anomalies. For example, success may hinge on a carefully built network of contacts. Such a network might lead an individual to refuse a promotion if such a promotion would destroy the network and move the person up but out.

In summary, career movement can be seen to occur along horizontal, lateral, and vertical lines, and career paths can be viewed as complex interactions of these three kinds of movement. People are highly sensitive to the kind of movement that job shifts represent because of their differing aspirations and self-images. The career anchor concept is one way of describing such self-images within the internal career.

4

Development of a Career Anchor

As a career evolves, the person develops a self-concept that includes some explicit answers to these questions:

1. What are my talents, skills, and areas of competence? What are my strengths and weaknesses?

2. What are my main motives, needs, drives, and goals in life? What do I want or not want, either because I have never wanted it or because I have reached a point of insight and no longer want it?

3. What are my values—the main criteria by which I judge what I am doing? Am I in an organization or job that is congruent with my values? How good do I feel about what I am doing? How proud or ashamed am I of my work and career?

This self-concept builds on whatever self-insight an individual has acquired from the experiences of youth and education. However, it cannot be a mature self-concept until a career occupant has had enough real occupational experience to know his or her talents, motives, and values. Such learning may require up to ten years or more of actual work experience. If the person has many varied experiences and gets meaningful feedback in each one, a self-concept develops more quickly. If a person has only a few jobs in the early years of the career or obtains minimal feedback, it may take much longer.

Talents, motives, and values become intertwined. People learn to be better at those things they value and are motivated to do, and they learn to value and be motivated by those things they happen to do well. They also gradually learn to avoid those things that they do not do well; although without clear feedback, they may cling to illusions about themselves that set them up for repeated failures. Talents without motivation gradually atrophy. Conversely, new challenges can reveal latent or hidden talents that simply had not had an opportunity to appear earlier.

People differ as to whether talents, motives, or values initially dominate their self-concepts and provide central themes to their careers. As time goes on, however, a need for congruence causes people to seek consistency and integration among the different elements of self-concept. How is this consistency learned? People first enter the world of work with many ambitions, hopes, fears, and illusions but with relatively little good information about themselves, especially about their abilities and talents. Through testing and counseling they get an idea of their interests, motives, and values as well as their intellectual and motor skills, but they cannot really determine how good they will be at a certain kind of work or how they will react to it emotionally.

Nowhere is this more true than in management, because of the difficulty of simulating some of its key skills and abilities. Until a person actually feels the responsibility of committing large sums of money, of hiring and firing people, of saying "no" to a valued subordinate, that person cannot tell whether he or she will be able to do it or will like doing it. This principle applies to many other occupations:

a person cannot tell if he or she has a talent in or likes the job without actually performing that job.

The early years in an occupation are a crucial time of learning—learning about the occupation or organization and learning about oneself in relation to the demands of the job. This process often is painful and full of surprises because of the many misconceptions and illusions with which people typically enter their early work situations. Many of people's dreams about who they are and what their work will be like may be inconsistent with their work experiences, causing "reality shock," a phenomenon that is observed in all occupations in the early years.

As people accumulate work experience, they have the opportunity to make choices; from these choices they begin to ascertain what they really find important. For each person, dominant themes emerge—critical skills or abilities that an individual wants to exercise or crucial needs or values that dominate one's orientation toward life. Previously, a person may have had a vague sense of these elements; but in the absence of actual life experience, he or she does not know how important they are or how any given talent, motive, or value relates in a subjective hierarchy to other elements of the total personality. Only when he or she is confronted with difficult choices does a person begin to decide what is really important to him or her.

With accumulation of work experience and feedback come clarification and insight, providing a basis for more rational and empowered career decisions. The self-concept begins to function more and more as a guidance system and as an anchor that constrains career choices. A person begins to have a sense of what is "me" and what is "not me." This knowledge keeps a person on course or in a safe harbor. As people recount their career choices, they increasingly refer to "being pulled back" to things they have strayed from or "figuring out" what they really want to do or "finding" themselves.

The career anchor, as defined here, is that one element in a person's self-concept that he or she will not give up, even in the face of difficult choices. People typically manage to fulfill a broad range of needs in any given career, but those needs are not all equally important. If all needs cannot be met, it is important to know which ones have highest priority.

A person's career anchor may not always match what he or she is doing occupationally because of external constraints over which the person has no control. For example, economic circumstances or family illness could prevent someone from pursuing something that his or her self-image dictates. If interviewed, that person would explain that what he or she currently is doing is "not really me, not really what I would like to be doing or am capable of doing." These are not just idle illusions talking; in many cases people have actualized their self-concepts the moment the external constraints were lifted.

The career anchor is the self-image; it can remain remarkably stable even without the opportunity to exercise it, as in the case of the starving artist who drives a cab. Self-image will change if the person obtains systematic experience and feedback that make it impossible to maintain an illusion, as in the case of the artist who repeatedly fails to produce art that meets even his or her own standards. However, self-image may not change if the constraint is seen as merely external and temporary.

Early in a career, each person confronts the issue of how to integrate work, family, and personal priorities. Some will decide to de-emphasize work, considering it merely instrumental to survival. For such a person, experience is shaped primarily by what might be called a "life anchor." For purposes of discussion, the focus here initially will be on those people for whom work and career are important enough to warrant speaking of career anchors. For many younger people the concept of life anchor may make more sense, and for many older people career commitments may be reassessed, decreasing the importance of career anchors.

Origin of the Concept "Career Anchor"

The concept of "career anchor" originally arose from a study designed to better understand how managerial careers evolved and how people learned the values and procedures of their employing organizations. A longitudinal study of forty-four alumni of the Master's program at the Sloan School of Management, Massachusetts Institute of Technology, began in 1961. The initial interviews and surveys of values and attitudes were conducted in 1961, 1962, and 1963 while the respondents were second-year students in the two-year Master's program. All were interviewed at their places of work six months after graduation and again one year after graduation. These interviews revealed a great deal about the problems of making the transition from school to work organizations.

All respondents completed questionnaires five years after graduation and had follow-up interviews in 1973, after they were approximately ten to twelve years into their careers. From these sources came insights into how the internal career evolves. The 1973 interviews elicited a detailed chronological career history, asking respondents not only to identify key choices and events but also to speculate about why they had made those particular choices and how they felt about each change. The interview format was essentially the same as that used in this book.

The actual events of the career histories proved to be highly varied, but the reasons that respondents gave for their choices and the pattern of their feelings about events proved to be surprisingly consistent. For each individual, underlying themes—of which he or she often had been unaware—reflected a growing sense of self, based on the learnings of the early years. When these people tried jobs that did not feel right to them, they referred to the image of being pulled back to something that fitted better— hence the metaphor of an anchor.

Types of Career Anchors

Based on this longitudinal study and on subsequent career-history interviews of several hundred people in various career stages, eight career anchor categories were identified:

- ✦ Technical/Functional Competence
- ✦ General Managerial Competence
- ✦ Autonomy/Independence
- ✦ Security/Stability
- ✦ Entrepreneurial Creativity
- ✦ Service/Dedication to a Cause
- ✦ Pure Challenge
- ✦ Lifestyle

Every person is concerned to some degree with each of these issues. The label "career anchor" indicates an area of such paramount importance to a person that he or she would not give it up. The person comes to define his or her basic self-image in terms of that concern, and it becomes an overriding issue at every stage of the career. To understand this concept fully, one needs to look at each of the anchors in greater detail and to highlight how people with divergent anchors differ from one another. The following descriptions of the eight anchors are intended to provide the reader with this information. Each description begins with the general characteristics of the anchor and then examines the issues involved in managing someone with that anchor, including the type of work, pay and benefits, promotion system, and recognition preferred by a person with that career anchor.

Technical/Functional Competence

Some people discover as their careers unfold that they have both a strong talent and high motivation for a particular kind of work. What really excites and motivates them is the exercise of their talent and the satisfaction of knowing that they are experts. This can happen in any kind of work. For example, an engineer may discover that he or she is very good at design; a salesperson may find real selling talent and desire; a manufacturing manager may encounter greater and greater pleasure in running complex plants; a financial analyst may uncover talent and enjoyment in solving complex capital-investment problems; a teacher may enjoy his or her growing expertise in the field; and so on.

As these people move along in their careers, they notice that if they are moved into other areas of work they are less satisfied and less skilled. They begin to feel pulled back to their areas of competence and enjoyment. They build a sense of identity around the *content* of their work—the technical or functional areas in which they are succeeding—and develop increased skills in those areas.

Technically/functionally anchored people commit themselves to a life of specialization and devalue the concerns of the general manager, although they are willing to be functional managers if it enables them to pursue their areas of expertise. Although most careers start out being technical/functional in their orientation and the early phase of most careers is involved with the development of a specialty, not everyone is excited by a specialty. For some people, the specialist job is a means to organizational membership or security more than it is an end in itself. For others, it is simply a steppingstone to higher rungs on the organizational ladder, a necessary step to get into general management. For still others, it is an opportunity to learn some skills that will be needed to launch into independent or entrepreneurial activities. Consequently, although most people start out specializing, only some find this intrinsically rewarding enough to develop career anchors around their specialties.

Type of work. The single most important characteristic of desirable work for members of this group is that it be challenging to them. If the work does not test their abilities and skills, it quickly becomes boring and demeaning and will result in their seeking other assignments. Because their self-esteem hinges on exercising talent, they need tasks that permit such exercise. Although others might be more concerned about the context of the work, this type of person is more concerned about the intrinsic *content* of the work.

Technical/functional people who have committed themselves to an organization (as opposed to an autonomous consultant) are willing and anxious to share in goal setting. However, once goals have been agreed on, they demand maximum autonomy in executing them. Not only do they want the autonomy in execution, but they generally also want unrestricted facilities, budgets, and resources of all kinds to enable them to perform the job appropriately. Conflict often emerges between general managers who are trying to limit the cost of specialized functions and the specialists who want to be able to spend whatever it takes to enable them to do the job properly.

The person anchored in this way will tolerate administrative or managerial work as long as he or she believes that it is essential to getting the job done; however, such work is viewed as painful and necessary rather than as intrinsically enjoyable or desirable. Being promoted into a more general job is viewed as totally undesirable by these people because it forces them out of the specialties with which they identify.

Talent for the interpersonal aspects of management varies in this group, resulting in the dilemma that if such people are promoted into supervisory positions and then discover that they have no talent for supervision, they typically are blocked organizationally. Most career ladders do not provide for easy return to the technical/functional staff role once a managerial job has been taken.

Finding a suitable role and challenging work as one progresses in a technical/functional career can be a difficult task, both for the individual and for the organization. Becoming more of a teacher and mentor to younger people is one workable solution. Careful redesign of work to take advantage of the experience level of the older specialist is another option, since this kind of person becomes something of a generalist within his or her technical area and is thus able to bring a broader perspective to problems.

Pay and benefits. Technical/functional people want to be paid for their skill levels, often defined by education and work experience. A person with a doctorate wants a higher salary than someone with a Master's degree, regardless of actual accomplishments. These people are oriented toward external equity, meaning that they will compare their salaries to what others of the same skill level earn in other organizations. Even if they are the highest-paid people in their own organizations, they will feel that they are not being treated fairly if they are underpaid compared with those in similar positions in other organizations.

Technical/functional people are oriented more toward absolute pay level than toward special incentives such as bonuses or stock options, except as forms of recognition. They probably prefer the type of benefit package that allows them to chose from a range of options—so-called "cafeteria" portable benefits—so they can choose the benefits they need (for instance, life insurance or retirement programs) because they view themselves as highly mobile and want to be able to take as much as possible with them. They are frightened of the "golden handcuffs" because they might get trapped in unchallenging work.

Promotion system. This group of people clearly prefers a professional promotional path that functions in parallel with the typical managerial path. They resent promotional systems that make advancement equivalent to moving into administration or management. Although this has been recognized in some research-and-development and engineering organizations, it is just as applicable to all the other functional specialties that exist in organizations (such as finance, marketing, manufacturing, or sales). Still, few organizations have developed career paths that are genuinely responsive to the needs of the technically/functionally anchored person.

Promotion for a technically/functionally anchored person does not necessarily have to be in terms of rank. If external market equity were achieved in salary, this person would respond to being awarded an increase in the scope of the job, to being allocated more resources or areas of responsibility, to being given a bigger budget or more technical support or subordinates, or to being consulted more on high-level decisions as a result of placement on key committees or task forces.

Type of recognition. The specialist values the recognition of his or her professional peers more than uninformed rewards from members of management. In other words, a compliment from a supervisor who really does not understand what was accomplished is worth less than acknowledgment from a professional peer or even from a subordinate who knows exactly what was accomplished and how difficult it might have been.

In terms of the type of recognition that is valued, at the top of the list is the opportunity for further learning and self-development in the specialty. Thus, educational opportunities, organization-sponsored sabbaticals, encouragement to attend professional meetings, budgets for buying books or equipment, and so on are highly valued. This is especially true because one of the greatest threats to technically/functionally anchored people as they age is obsolescence.

In addition to continuing education, this group values formal recognition through being identified to colleagues and other members of the organization as valued specialists. Prizes, awards, publicity, and other public acknowledgments are more important than an extra percentage in the paycheck, provided that the base pay is perceived as equitable in the first place.

The technically/functionally anchored person is most vulnerable to organizational mismanagement, because organizational careers tend to be designed by general managers who value learning several functions, achieving internal equity in pay, forging organizational loyalty, and getting along with all kinds of people. All of these things may be irrelevant to the technical/functional person. If this person is a valued resource in the organization, some redesign of the career development system typically will be needed.

General Managerial Competence

Some people—but only some—discover as their careers progress that they really want to become general managers, that management per se interests them, that they have the range of competence that is required to be a general manager, and that they have the ambition to rise to organizational levels where they will be responsible for major policy decisions and where their own efforts will make the difference between success and failure.

Members of this group differ from the technical/functional people in that they view specialization as a trap. They recognize the necessity to know several functional areas well and they accept that one must be expert in one's business or industry to function well in a general manager's job. Key values and motives for this group of people are advancement up the corporate hierarchy to higher levels of responsibility, opportunities for leadership, contributions to the success of their organizations, and high income.

When they first enter organizations, most people have aspirations to get ahead in some general sense. Many of them talk explicitly of ambitions to rise to the top, but few have a realistic picture of what is actually required in the way of talents, motives, and values to make it to the top. With experience it becomes clearer, especially to those who have committed themselves to general management as a career, that they need not only a high level of motivation to reach the top but also a mixture of talents and skills in the following three basic areas:

Analytical competence: The ability to identify, to analyze, to synthesize, and to solve problems under conditions of incomplete information and uncertainty. General managers point out the importance of being able to decipher what is going on; to cut through a mass of possibly irrelevant detail to get to the heart of a matter; to judge the reliability and validity of information in the absence of clear verification opportunities; and, in the end, to pose the problem or question in such a way that it can be worked on. Financial, marketing, technological, human, and other elements have to be combined into problem statements that are relevant to the future success of the organization.

It is commonly said that general managers are decision makers. However, it is probably more accurate to say that general managers are capable of identifying and stating problems in such a way that decisions can be made. General managers manage the decision-making process; to do this they must be able to think cross-functionally and integratively. Such thinking requires other competencies.

Interpersonal and intergroup competence: The ability to influence, supervise, lead, handle, and control people at all levels of the organization toward organizational goal achievement. General managers point out that this skill involves eliciting valid information from others, getting others to collaborate to achieve synergistic outcomes, motivating people to contribute what they know to the problem-solving process, communicating clearly the goals to be achieved, facilitating the decision-making process and implementation, monitoring progress, and instituting corrective action if necessary.

Much of the technical information that goes into decision making increasingly is in the hands of subordinates and peers with technical/functional career anchors. Therefore, the quality of decisions largely hinges on the ability of general managers to bring the right people together for problem-solving purposes and then to create a climate that will elicit full exchange of information and full commitment from these people. More and more, such decision making occurs in groups because the complexity of the problems requires that people share information in order to solve problems. Thus, group skills are very relevant for general managers.

New managers often wonder whether or not they will be any good at supervising others and, of almost equal importance, whether they will like supervising. Most new managers do not know what interpersonal skills they have or need unless they have been in leadership roles in school. Thus, management recruiters are anxious to know about extracurricular activities when they assess a candidate. A good record in this area is of great value, both to the individual and the organization. Once a new manager has had an opportunity to test himself or herself and finds that the interpersonal work is manageable and enjoyable, self-confidence and ambition increase rapidly.

People who discover either that they are not talented in supervision or that they do not really like that kind of work gravitate toward other pursuits and build their career anchors around technical/functional competence, autonomy, or even entrepreneurial activity. It is crucial for organizations to create career systems that make it possible for such people to move out of supervisory roles if they are not suited to such roles, preferably without penalty. All too often the best engineer or salesperson is promoted to be a supervisor, only to fail in the role but then to be stuck in it, to the inevitable detriment of his or her career and the company.

Emotional competence: The capacity to be stimulated by emotional and interpersonal issues and crises rather than to be exhausted or debilitated by them; the capacity to bear high levels of responsibility without becoming paralyzed; and the ability to exercise power and make difficult decisions without guilt or shame. All of the general managers interviewed referred to the painful process of learning to make tough decisions, and almost all of them said that they had not anticipated what it would be like or how they would react. Only as they gained confidence in their abilities to handle their own feelings did they gain confidence that they could really succeed as general managers. They cited examples such as laying off a valued older employee; deciding between two programs, each backed by valued subordinates; committing large sums of money to a project, knowing that the fate of many people depended on success or failure; asking a subordinate to perform a very difficult job that he or she might not want to do; inspiring a demoralized organization; fighting for a project at a higher level; delegating to subordinates and leaving them alone enough to learn how to do things; and taking ownership of a decision, in the sense of being accountable even without control of its implementation.

Most general managers report that such decisions occur continually and that one of the most difficult aspects of the job is functioning day after day without giving up, getting an ulcer, or having a nervous breakdown. The essence of the general manager's job is to absorb the emotional strains of uncertainty, interpersonal conflict, and responsibility. It is this aspect of the job that often repels the technically/functionally anchored individual but excites and motivates the managerially anchored individual.

General managers differ from people with other anchors primarily in that they have analytical competence, interpersonal and intergroup competence, and emotional competence. They cannot function without some degree of each of these areas of competence, although no one area has to be developed to a very high level. The combination of skills is what is essential for the general manager, while the technical/functional person needs high development of one skill element. General managers are quite different in these respects from functional managers, and it takes longer to learn to be a general manager because these competencies can be learned only through actual experiences.

Type of work. Managerially anchored people want high levels of responsibility; challenging, varied, and integrative work; leadership opportunities; and opportunities to contribute to the success of their organizations. They will measure the attractiveness of a work assignment in terms of its importance to the success of the organization, and they will identify strongly with the organization and its success or failure as a measure of how well they have done. In a sense, then, they are real "organization people" whose identities rest on having effective organizations to manage.

Pay and benefits. Managerially anchored people measure themselves by their income levels and expect to be very highly paid. In contrast to the technically/functionally anchored people, they are oriented more toward internal equity than external equity. They want to be paid substantially more than the level below them and will be satisfied if that condition is met, even if someone at their own level in another company is earning more. They also want short-term rewards such as bonuses for achieving organizational targets; and because they are identified with the organization, they are very responsive to things such as stock options that give them a sense of ownership and shared fate.

Managerially anchored people share with security-oriented people a willingness (if not a positive desire) for the "golden handcuffs," particularly in the form of good retirement benefits. So much of a managerially anchored person's career is tied up with a given company that his or her particular skills may not be portable in mid-life or later. However, an increasing number of general managers now shift from company to company and take their benefit packages with them or negotiate for equivalent packages. Since intimate knowledge of a particular industry and company are important to the decision-making process, it is not clear whether such movement can be successful. It is possible that new specialties are arising within general management itself, such as the "turn-around manager" who is brought into a failing company from outside to get it back to a profitable status, or the "start-up manager" whose specialty is to open new parts of the organization in overseas locations or to develop new products or markets.

Promotion system. Managerially anchored people insist on promotion based on merit, measured performance, and results. Even though they acknowledge that personality, style, seniority, politics, and other factors play a role in determining promotions, general managers believe that the ability to get results is the critical criterion. All other factors are legitimate only because they are essential to getting results.

Type of recognition. The most important forms of recognition for managerially anchored people are promotions to positions of higher responsibility. They measure such positions by a combination of rank, title, salary, number of subordinates, and size of budget, as well as by less tangible factors defined by their superiors (such as the importance of a given project, department, or division to the future of the company). They expect promotions frequently. If they are too long in particular jobs, they assume that they are not performing adequately. Every organization seems to have a timetable for promotions, and managers measure their successes partly by whether they are moving in accordance with their organizations' timetables. Thus, movement itself becomes an important form of recognition unless it is clearly lateral or downward.

Organizations sometimes develop implicit career paths that become known informally to the more ambitious general managers. It may be commonly understood, for example, that one should move from finance to marketing, then take over a staff function in an overseas company, then move to headquarters, and eventually take over a division. If promotions do not follow the typical path, these people will worry that they are "off the fast track" (not being considered seriously as having higher managerial talent) and are losing their potential. For this reason, movement to the right job is another important form of recognition.

This group of people is highly responsive to monetary recognition in the form of raises, bonuses, and stock options; they enjoy titles, status symbols (such as large offices, automobiles, or special privileges), and, most importantly, the approval of their superiors. Whereas the technically/functionally anchored person only values approval from someone who really understands his or her work, general managers value approval specifically from the superiors who control their most important incentive—promotion to the next higher level.

In summary, the person who is anchored in managerial competence and who therefore aspires to a position in general management has a very different orientation from others in the typical organization, even though he or she may start in a very similar kind of job. Interviews disclosed that such an orientation developed as soon as the person had enough data to determine whether or not he or she had the analytical, interpersonal, and emotional skills to be a general manager. Some people had these insights early and if the organizations did not respond to their needs to rise quickly, they went to other organizations that permitted them to reach responsible levels at a rapid pace.

Autonomy/Independence

Some people discover early in their working lives that they cannot stand to be bound by other people's rules, procedures, working hours, dress codes, and other norms that almost invariably arise in any kind of organization. Regardless of what they work on, such people have an overriding need to do things in their own way, at their own pace, and according to their own standards. They find organizational life to be restrictive, irrational, and intrusive into their private lives; therefore, they prefer to pursue more independent careers on their own terms. If forced to make a choice between a present job that permits autonomy and a much better job that requires giving it up, the autonomy/independence-anchored person would stay in his or her present job.

Everyone has needs for certain levels of autonomy, which vary during the course of life. For some people, however, such needs come to be overriding; they feel that they must be masters of their own ships at all times. Sometimes extreme autonomy needs result from high levels of education and professionalism, in which the educational process itself teaches the person to be totally self-reliant and responsible. Sometimes such feelings are developed in childhood by child-rearing methods that put great emphasis on self-reliance and independent judgment.

People who begin to organize their careers around such needs gravitate toward autonomous professions. If interested in business or management, they may go into consulting or teaching. Or they may end up in areas of work in which autonomy is relatively possible even in large organizations—research and development, field sales offices, data processing, market research, financial analysis, or the management of geographically remote units.

Type of work. The autonomy-anchored person prefers clearly delineated, time-bound kinds of work within his or her area of expertise. Contract or project work, whether part-time, full-time, or even temporary, is acceptable and often desirable. In addition, this type of person wants work that clearly defines goals but leaves the means of accomplishment up to him or her. The autonomy-anchored person cannot stand close supervision; he or she might agree to organization-imposed goals or targets but wants to be left alone after those goals are set.

Pay and benefits. The autonomy-anchored person is terrified of the "golden handcuffs." He or she would prefer merit pay for performance, immediate payoffs, bonuses, and other forms of compensation with no limitations or obligations attached. People anchored in autonomy prefer portable benefits and a choice-type benefit package that permits them to select the options most suitable to their life situations at given points in time.

Promotion system. This type of person responds most to promotions that reflect past accomplishments; he or she wants a new job to have even more freedom than the previous one. In other words, promotion comes to mean more autonomy. Being given more rank or responsibility can actually threaten an autonomy-anchored person if it entails loss of autonomy. An autonomous sales representative knows that to become sales manager might mean less freedom, so he or she often turns down such promotions.

Type of recognition. The autonomy-anchored person responds best to forms of recognition that are portable. Medals, testimonials, letters of commendation, prizes, awards, and other such rewards probably mean more than promotions, title changes, or even financial bonuses.

Most organizational reward systems are not at all geared to dealing with the autonomy-anchored person. Therefore, such people often leave in disgust, complaining about organizational limitations and rules. If their talents are not needed, no harm is done. But if key people in the organization have autonomy anchors, it becomes important to redesign personnel systems to make organizational life more palatable to these people. Such job redesign is particularly difficult because most systems are not geared for dealing with contract or part-time work, the form of work that is most attractive to the autonomy-anchored person.

Security/Stability

Some people have an overriding need to organize their careers so that they feel safe and secure, so that future events are predictable, and so that they can relax and feel successful. Everyone needs some degree of security and stability throughout life; at certain life stages financial security can become the overriding issue, such as when one is raising and educating a family or approaching retirement. For some people security and stability are predominant throughout their careers to the point that these concerns guide and constrain all major career decisions.

Such people often seek jobs in organizations that provide job tenure, that have the reputation of avoiding layoffs, that have good retirement plans and benefit programs, and that have the image of being strong and reliable. For this reason, government and civil service jobs are often attractive to these people. They obtain some of their self-satisfaction from identifying with their organizations even if they do not have high-ranking or important jobs.

Security/stability-anchored people welcome the "golden handcuffs" and are usually willing to give responsibility for their career management to their employers. In exchange for tenure they are willing to be told what work to do, how much to travel, where to live, how often to switch assignments, and so on. Because of this, they are sometimes perceived as lacking ambition or may be looked on with disdain in cultures that place a high value on ambition and achievement. This can be an unfair stereotype, because some of these individuals have risen from humble origins into fairly high-level managerial positions. When they reach middle management in large corporations, they genuinely feel that they have succeeded because of where they started socio-economically.

The highly talented among this group reach high levels in organizations, but they prefer jobs that require steady, predictable performance. The less talented may level off in middle management or in staff jobs and gradually become less involved. If they obtain the security they are seeking, they are content with whatever levels they have attained. If they have unused talents, they are content to find nonwork or noncareer activities in which they can exercise those talents.

Type of work. Security/stability-anchored people prefer stable, predictable work and are more concerned about the context of the work than the nature of the work itself. Job enrichment, job challenge, and other intrinsic motivational tools do not matter as much to them as improved pay, working conditions, and benefits. Much organizational work has this character, and every organization is highly dependent on having among its employees a large number of people anchored in security and in technical/functional competence.

Pay and benefits. The person who is primarily anchored in security/stability prefers to be paid in steadily predictable increments based on length of service. Such a person prefers benefit packages that emphasize insurance and retirement programs.

Promotion system. The security/stability-anchored person prefers a seniority-based promotion system and welcomes a published grade and rank system that delineates how long one must serve in any given grade before promotion can be expected. Obviously this kind of person relishes a formal tenure system such as is found in schools and universities.

Type of recognition. The security/stability-anchored person wants to be recognized for his or her loyalty and steady performance, preferably with reassurances of further stability and continued employment. Above all, this person needs to believe that loyalty makes a real contribution to the organization's performance. Most personnel systems are well geared to this kind of person, although guarantees of tenure are rare.

Entrepreneurial Creativity

Some people discover early in life that they have an overriding need to create new businesses of their own by developing new products or services, by building new organizations through financial manipulation, or by taking over existing businesses and reshaping them to their own specifications. These are not necessarily only inventors or creative artists, although some of them become entrepreneurs. Nor should these people be confused with creative researchers, market analysts, or advertising executives. The creative urge in this group is specifically toward creating new organizations, products, or services that can be identified closely with the entrepreneur's own efforts, that will survive on their own, and that will be economically successful. Making money is then a measure of success.

Many people dream about forming their own businesses and express those dreams at various stages of their careers. In some cases these dreams express needs for autonomy and to get out on one's own. However, entrepreneurially anchored people typically began to pursue these dreams relentlessly early in life, often having started small money-making enterprises even during secondary school. They found that they had both the talent and an extraordinarily high level of motivation to prove to the world that they could do it. Such motivation often derived from their own families, which previously may have produced successful entrepreneurs. They did not stay with traditional organizations very long, or they kept organizational jobs while their real energies went into the building of their own enterprises.

It is important to distinguish this career anchor from the autonomy/independence one. Many people want to run their own businesses because of autonomy needs. What distinguishes entrepreneurs is their obsession with proving that they can create businesses. This obsession often means sacrificing both autonomy and stability, particularly in the early stages before a business is successful. Other entrepreneurially oriented people consistently fail at entrepreneurism, spending the greater part of their careers searching for creative solutions while making a living at conventional jobs. For example, a person may be a sales representative or a middle manager in some enterprise while trying to build a real-estate empire or looking for a company to acquire and run in his or her spare time. What makes such a person an "entrepreneur" is the dedication to creating the new enterprise and the willingness to drop a pre-existing job once a venture has been located.

Type of work. Entrepreneurially anchored people are obsessed with the need to create, and they tend to become bored easily. In their own enterprises, they may continue to invent new products or services, or they may lose interest, sell these enterprises, and start new ones. They are restless and continually require new creative challenges.

Pay and benefits. For this group of people, ownership is ultimately the most important issue. Often they do not pay themselves very well, but they retain control of their organizations' stock. If they develop new products, they want to own the patents. Large organizations that attempt to retain entrepreneurs often misunderstand the intensity of these needs. Unless he or she is given control of the new enterprise, with patents and 51 percent of the stock, an entrepreneurially anchored person will not stay with an organization. Entrepreneurs want to accumulate wealth, not so much for its own sake but as a way of showing the world what they have accomplished. Benefit packages are probably not a meaningful issue to them.

Promotion system. Entrepreneurs want a system that permits them to be wherever they need to be at any given point during their careers. They want the power and the freedom to move into the roles they consider to be key and to meet their own needs. Usually these roles are ones that permit them to continue to exercise creativity, such as head of research and development or chairman of the board of directors.

Type of recognition. Building fortunes and sizeable enterprises are two of the most important ways in which members of this group achieve recognition. In addition, entrepreneurs are rather self-centered, seeking high personal visibility and public recognition. Often they display this quality by putting their own names on products or companies.

Sense of Service, Dedication to a Cause

Some people enter occupations because of central values that they want to embody in their work. They are oriented more toward these values than toward the actual talents or areas of competence involved. Their career decisions are based on the desire to improve the world in some fashion. Those in the helping professions—such as medicine, nursing, social work, teaching, and the ministry—are typically considered to hold this career anchor. However, dedication to a cause clearly also characterizes some people in business management and in organizational careers. Some examples include the human resource specialist who works on affirmative action programs, the labor lawyer intent on improving labor-management relations, the research scientist working on a new drug, or the manager who chooses to go into public service in order to improve some aspect of society. Values such as working with people, serving humanity, and helping one's nation can be powerful anchors in one's career.

However, not everyone in a service-oriented occupation is motivated by the desire to serve. Some doctors, lawyers, ministers, and social workers may be anchored in technical/functional competence or autonomy or security; some may want to become general managers. Without knowing which anchor is actually operating, one will not know what the career occupant really wants.

Type of work. Service-anchored persons clearly want work that permits them to influence their employing organizations or social policies in the direction of their values. A good example of this person is a professor of agriculture who left a tenured university position to accept a job as manager of environmental planning for a large mining company. He stated that he would continue to work for the company as long as he was allowed to do key environmental planning and to have the power to get things done.

Pay and benefits. People anchored in sense of service or dedication to a cause want fair pay for their contributions and portable benefits because they have no a priori organizational loyalty. Money per se is not central to them.

Promotion system. More important than monetary rewards is a promotional system that recognizes the contribution of the service-anchored person and moves him or her into positions with more influence and the freedom to operate autonomously.

Type of recognition. Service-anchored people want recognition and support both from their professional peers and from their superiors; they want to feel that their values are shared by higher levels of management. In the absence of such support, they move toward more autonomous professions such as consulting.

Pure Challenge

Some people anchor their careers in the perception that they can conquer anything and anybody. They define success as overcoming impossible obstacles, solving unsolvable problems, or winning out over extremely tough opponents. As they progress, they seek ever-tougher challenges. For some, this takes the form of seeking jobs in which they face more and more difficult problems. However, these people are not technically/functionally anchored because they seem not to care in what area the problem occurs. Some high-level strategy/management consultants seem to fit this pattern in that they relish more and more difficult kinds of strategic assignments.

For others, the challenge is defined in interpersonal and competitive terms. For example, some naval aviators perceive their sole purpose in life to be to prepare themselves for the ultimate confrontation with an enemy (Derr, 1986). In that confrontation these "warriors" would prove to themselves and to the world their superiority in competitive combat. Although the military version of this anchor may seem somewhat overdramatized, other people also define life in competitive terms. Many salespeople, professional athletes, and even some managers define their careers essentially as daily combat or competition in which winning is everything.

Most people seek a certain level of challenge; for the person anchored in pure challenge, it is the thing that matters most. The area of work, the kind of employing organization, the pay system, the type of promotion system, and the forms of recognition are all subordinate to whether or not the job provides constant opportunities for self-tests. In the absence of such constant tests of self, the person becomes bored and irritable. Often such people talk about the importance of variety in their careers; one reason some of them are attracted to general management is the variety and intense challenge that managerial situations provide.

The managerial issues involved in motivating and developing such people are intrinsically complex. On the one hand, these people are already highly motivated to develop themselves and probably are very loyal to organizations that give them adequate opportunities for self-tests. But they also can be very single-minded and certainly can make life difficult for those who do not have comparable aspirations. The 1979 Hollywood film *The Great Santini* depicted the problems created by a "warrior," both for his supervisors and for his family. A career for such a person has meaning only if competitive skill can be exercised; if there is no such opportunity, the person can become demoralized and become a problem to himself and others.

Lifestyle

At first glance this concept seems like a contradiction in terms. People who organize their existence around lifestyle are, in one sense, saying that their careers are less important to them and, therefore, that they do not have a career anchor. They belong in a discussion of career anchors, however, because a growing number of people who are highly motivated toward meaningful careers are, at the same time, adding the condition that the career must be integrated with total lifestyle. This is not merely a matter of balancing personal and professional lives as many people traditionally have done; it is more a matter of finding a way to integrate the needs of the individual, the family, and the career.

Because such an integration is itself an evolving function, this kind of person wants flexibility more than anything else. Unlike the autonomy-anchored person who wants flexibility, those with lifestyle anchors are quite willing to work for organizations provided that the right options are available at the right time. Such options might include traveling or moving only at times when family situations permit, part-time work if life concerns require it, sabbaticals, paternity and maternity leaves, day-care options (which are becoming especially relevant for the growing population of dual-career couples and single parents), flexible working hours, work at home during normal working hours, and so on. Lifestyle-anchored people look more for an organizational attitude than a specific program—an attitude that reflects respect for personal and family concerns and that makes genuine renegotiation of the psychological contract possible.

This anchor was first observed in women graduates of the Massachusetts Institute of Technology Sloan School of Management but increasingly is being observed in male graduates, especially those who have gone into management and strategy consulting. It probably reflects a number of trends in society and is an inevitable effect of the dual-career family. What it requires most from managers is understanding, because it is not clear what particular organizational responses will be most helpful in any given case, except that policies and career systems in general must become more flexible.

One specific lifestyle issue is the growing unwillingness of career occupants to move geographically. At first this seemed to be an aspect of the security anchor, but it has become increasingly clear that people who are unwilling to move feel this way less for security/stability reasons than for reasons of integrating personal, family, and career issues. This trend, if it continues, could have major implications for the external career path. Many companies take it for granted that people will move when asked to do so and treat this as a positive developmental career step. If organizations encounter more and more people anchored in lifestyle, it is not clear whether these people will have to sacrifice career advancement or whether their companies will redefine career paths to make advancement more feasible within a confined geographical area.

Are There Other Career Anchors?

Research to date indicates that most people can be described in terms of the eight anchors presented. These anchors have been found in a variety of occupations and apply equally well to doctors, lawyers, teachers, naval officers, consultants, police officers, and even production workers (if they are observed off the job). Even "nonpaying" occupations such as homemaking can be seen in terms of the different anchors; spouses of career-involved people find that they enjoy homemaking for reasons that mirror the anchor categories.

People often ask if there are other anchors, especially ones centered around power, variety, pure creativity, or organizational identity. According to the research guideline used, if two or more cases absolutely did not fit the existing eight categories and clearly resembled each other in some dimension, an additional anchor category would be created. Thus far, each proposed dimension has proved to be an aspect of another anchor or has been expressed differently in different anchor groups.

Power and creativity, for example, seem to be universal needs and are expressed in different ways by different anchor groups. The technical/functional person expresses power through superior knowledge and skill; the entrepreneur through building an organization; the general manager through obtaining a position that provides rank, influence, and resources; the service-oriented person through moral persuasion; and so on. Similarly, creativity can be displayed in each of the anchor categories in different ways.

Variety is something else that many people want and thrive on, but it is not an anchor per se because it can be obtained through autonomy, managerial challenges, entrepreneurial activity, or lifestyle. Only those anchored in technical/functional competence, security, and service trade some aspects of variety for other important considerations in their career evolution.

From the point of view of this exercise in self-analysis, a person should attempt to locate his or her true anchor but also should allow for the possibility of having a different pattern from any of the ones described. It is important to become more aware of one's patterns of talents, motives, and values, even if they do not fit exactly in the categories described. What people must find out about themselves is what they would not give up if forced to make a choice; that is the true career anchor.

Can a Person Have More Than One Anchor?

A career anchor is defined as the *one* thing a person would not give up if forced to make a choice. This definition allows for only one anchor—the one set of talents, values, and motives at the top of one's personal hierarchy. However, many career situations make it possible to fulfill several sets of talents, motives, and values, making a choice unnecessary and thus preventing a person from finding out what is really at the top of his or her hierarchy. For example, a functional manager in a paternalistic company simultaneously can fulfill security, autonomy, technical/functional, managerial, and even lifestyle anchors. In order to determine an anchor, that person must then invent hypothetical career options that would force a choice. For example, would that person choose to be a division general manager or the chief corporate officer in his or her function? Most people can identify their true anchors if they pose such choice situations to themselves.

If no anchor emerges clearly, another possibility is that the person has not had enough life experience to develop priorities that determine how to make those choices. People in this situation would benefit from determining what anchors are highest and exploring their reactions to different situations through systematic job choices. For example, a person may not know whether he or she has a talent or taste for general management in the absence of opportunities in that area. This person might volunteer to run a project, become a committee chairperson, ask to be acting manager of a unit, or try to get experience in some other way. In lieu of such experiences, he or she might find people who are clearly in that kind of job and interview them in detail about what it is like to be in that situation.

Do Anchors Change?

As yet all evidence is not in as to whether or not anchors change. Too few people have been studied for long enough periods of time to determine how career anchors evolve. However, fifteen of the original panelists have been followed into their mid-forties; thus far, the weight of evidence is on the side of stability. One would expect this because as people clarify their self-images—as they become more aware of what they are good at, want, and value—they tend to want to hold on to those self-images. The better people know themselves, the more they want to hold on to those insights.

Consider the following examples:

+ A technically/functionally anchored engineering manager in a large corporation found himself moving toward general management because of the nature of the external career path. Because he sensed that his next promotion would be to a generalist job, he began to lobby among his friends in senior management to be assigned to a high-level staff job at headquarters, and he successfully created this lateral move. He was willing to give up a promotion to a higher-level general-management job to remain in his preferred technical area.

+ Another technical/functional manager resigned because his job was boring to him and he was dead-ended. He then picked up his career as a successful consultant in that same technical/functional area. His career changed, but his anchor did not.

+ An autonomy-anchored individual dropped out of organizational life altogether and lived a marginal life until he got married and had children. Instead of returning to the mainstream, he and his wife opened an antique shop that permitted him to remain autonomous.

+ Each of two unsuccessful entrepreneurs has not yet found an enterprise to develop and is living a marginal life while searching for an enterprise, rather than settling for a more secure existence. One successful entrepreneur lost all of his wealth some years ago and is now starting up a whole new series of enterprises.

Some people who make dramatic mid-life changes in their external careers are trying to actualize what were their anchors all along; they simply never had the chance to do what they really wanted to do. For example, a computer consultant with a technical/functional anchor who had always wanted to go to law school finally did so when a small inheritance enabled him to finance it. Following graduation, he drifted into practicing law in a small town and developed a successful practice using many of the computer and consulting skills he had acquired. He remained anchored in the technological/functional area.

Because of the way that careers are structured, one's job and one's career anchor often do not match. A technically/functionally anchored person might be promoted to general manager, or a managerially anchored person might be given a high-level staff job. A security-anchored person might be convinced to join an entrepreneurial venture, or an autonomy-oriented person might take a boring but stable job under a repressive boss to earn money. People are able to perform somewhat in such situations, but they are not happy and do not feel that their real selves are engaged. They can adapt to circumstances and make the best of them, but their anchors do not change; as soon as there is an opportunity, they will seek a better match.

Conclusion: Matching Individual and Organizational Needs

The individual, internal side of the career has been explored in some detail by focusing on career stages, on how career movement and success can be analyzed, and on how the concept of career anchors sheds light on the self-images that people develop as their careers evolve. It is essential for the individual career occupant to develop insight about his or her career anchor in order to make better career plans and choices.

At the same time, as people gain insights into their own careers, they can use these insights to better manage the careers of others. In other words, the ultimate issue of career development is matching the needs of the individual with those of the organization. What complicates this process is that individuals are very different from one another, as shown by career anchor research. At the same time, organizations differ from one another, and their needs change as the environments in which they operate change. Matching two dynamic processes of this sort is, at best, difficult.

Who is to be responsible for such matching? Obviously it needs to be a shared responsibility among individual career occupants, the employing organizations and managers, and other institutions such as universities and government agencies.

What Can the Individual Career Occupant Do?

The primary responsibility of the career occupant is self-insight and the sharing of such insights with the relevant career manager in the employing organization. If an individual does not know his or her needs and biases, the career cannot be managed constructively. The individual must communicate clearly with the organization and make intelligent choices. It is unrealistic to expect managers and organizations to understand employees well enough to make valid career decisions for them (although this is how most career systems work at the present time). Ultimately people must learn to manage their own careers.

What Can Organizations and Managers Do?

Organizations and managers can begin with the following three suggestions:

1. *Create more flexible career paths, incentive systems, and reward systems.* Such systems can accommodate the needs of a variety of career occupants, even those in the same job category.

2. *Stimulate more self-insight and self-management.* Managers should analyze their own career anchors and manage their own careers more closely, thereby serving as role models for their subordinates.

3. *Clarify what the organization needs from the individual career occupant.* Organizations should do a better job of analyzing the specific characteristics of different jobs to be performed in any given career and should communicate them clearly to career seekers and job incumbents. If a person knows himself or herself well but cannot get good information about the tasks required for a given job, he or she cannot make an intelligent choice. If the organization is to put the right talent in the right place, it must be clearer about what it needs, by means of a better job/role-planning process.

What Can Other Institutions Do?

Inevitably in some situations the match between the individual and the organization is impossible because the talents do not match the requirements, because the organization has a surplus of people, or because the person cannot get along in a particular kind of organization. The most common version of this dilemma is when a change in technology makes large numbers of employees "obsolete." Many organizations create retraining and redeployment opportunities to minimize negative impacts, but often some people cannot be retrained or are surplus. In such instances, some other institution, supported either by the government or by industry consortia, must provide a safety net or transition cushion to allow those people to get new education and training. In other words, displaced workers must be made economically secure for at least two to three years while they redefine career focus and learn new skills. Technologies are changing more rapidly, so the building of such institutions for the management of career transition will become increasingly important.

Only if the organization, the individual career occupant, and other institutions work together to improve the matching process over the length of an entire career is there a chance to maximize both organizational performance and individual satisfaction. This is the challenge for the future.

5

Career Anchor Interview

T he next step is to have your partner interview you about past, present, and future career events, starting with your education. The actual questions are written on the next several pages; room is provided for your partner to write down notes based on what you say. You and your partner should both read this page to become acquainted with the interview process.

The interview focuses on the actual choices you have made and plan to make in the future. For each major decision or action taken, you are asked to explore why you made that decision or took that action and how you felt about it. The interview is deliberately historical and will help you reconstruct your past choices so that you can explore the patterns and your reasons for making these choices. It is the patterns that you and your partner should listen for as the interview progresses.

As you get into the interview, both you and your partner can feel free to go beyond the questions provided and probe other areas. However, it is recommended that you stay with the format of asking "What did you do or decide?" before you ask "Why?" or "How did you feel about it?"

Please give this booklet to your partner at this point.

Interview Questions

The purpose of the interview is to help you and your partner to understand the factors that guide and constrain careers by identifying patterns or themes in events and the reasons behind them. Work through the questions in a relaxed manner and feel free to deviate to other related issues that may come up. Your job is to help your partner to talk out his or her career history so that you can examine its patterns and themes together.

1. *Education.* Let's start with your education. What did you concentrate on in school? (Explore especially university and postgraduate education.)

   Why did you choose those areas?

   How do you feel now about having chosen those areas?

2. *First Job.* What was your first real job after your educa-tion? (If you *did not* start out working, what was your first major life event after your education?)

What were you looking for in your first job or life event? Why did you make that choice?

3. *Goals.* What were your ambitions or long-range goals when you started your career?

How did the first job work out in terms of your goals?

4. *Next Job or Major Life Event.* What was your first major change in your job or employing organization?

How did this come about? Who initiated the change? What were the reasons for the change?

How did you feel about the change? How did it relate to your goals?

5. *Next Job or Major Life Event.* What was the next major change in your job or employer?

How did this come about? Who initiated the change? What were the reasons for the change?

How did you feel about the change? How did it relate to your goals?

6. Continue to analyze what you consider to be the major changes in your job, organization, career, or life. List each change and analyze the reasons as well as the consequences.

Next Job (or Career or Life Change):

How did this come about? Who initiated the change? What were the reasons for the change?

How did you feel about the change? How did it relate to your goals?

7. Next Job (or Career or Life Change):

How did this come about? Who initiated the change? What were the reasons for the change?

How did you feel about the change? How did it relate to your goals?

8. *Next Job (or Career or Life Change):*

How did this come about? Who initiated the change? What were the reasons for the change?

How did you feel about the change? How did it relate to your goals?

Continue to analyze job/career/life changes until the present, using the preceding format of questions. Use blank paper if necessary.

9. As you look back over your career and life so far, do you see any major transition points, times when the change seemed more than routine? Please describe each of these times.

What was the transition? How did it come about? Who initiated it?

How did you feel about it? How was it related to your goals?

10. Using the same format, describe other major transitions. Use extra blank paper if necessary.

11. As you look back over your career and life so far, can you describe some times that you especially enjoyed?

    What was it about those times that made them enjoyable?

12. Were there times that you especially did not enjoy?

    What was it about those times that made them not enjoyable?

13. Have you ever refused a job or a promotion? If yes, can you describe it?

Why did you refuse it?

As you look ahead in your career, are there things you would like especially to avoid? Are there things you are afraid of?

What about these things makes you want to avoid them or makes you afraid?

14. Have your ambitions or long-range goals changed since you started your career? When? Why?

How would you now describe your long-range goals?

15. As you look ahead in your career, what are the things you are especially looking forward to?

Why are you looking forward to these things?

What do you think your next job will be?

After that what do you think your next job will be?

(Continue asking for next jobs until you elicit the answer to what the person would "ultimately" like to be.)

16. What do you think will actually happen in the next ten years of your career?

Why do you think this?

17. How would you describe your occupation to others?

What are you really good at?

What do you most want out of your career?

What values do you especially try to uphold in your career?

Do you have any other comments about yourself that you would like to make at this point?

18. As you think over the answers you have given, what patterns or themes do you see?

What inconsistencies, contradictions, or conflicts do you see in what you have identified?

What hypothetical situations might resolve those conflicts or inconsistencies?

Let's go on now to look at possible career anchor categories.

At this point the interviewer should return the booklet to the person being interviewed.

Identifying Your Career Anchor

The descriptions below are reminders of the career anchor categories presented in Chapter 4. If the short descriptions are too general, go back to the categories in the text to refresh your memory.

Technical/Functional Competence

If your career anchor is competence in some technical or functional area, what you would not give up is the opportunity to apply your skills in that area and to continue to develop those skills to an ever higher level. You derive your sense of identity from the exercise of your skills and are most happy when your work permits you to be challenged in those areas. You may be willing to manage others in your technical or functional area, but you are not interested in management for its own sake and would avoid general management because you would have to leave your own area of expertise. Your inventory score in this area is in the first column of the scoring sheet under TF.

General Managerial Competence

If your career anchor is general managerial competence, what you would not give up is the opportunity to climb to a level high enough in an organization to enable you to integrate the efforts of others across functions and to be responsible for the output of a particular unit of the organization. You want to be responsible and accountable for total results and you identify your own work with the success of the organization for which you work. If you are presently in a technical or functional area, you view that as a necessary learning experience; however, your ambition is to get to a generalist job as soon as possible. Being at a high managerial level in a function does not interest you. Your inventory score in this area is in the second column of the scoring sheet under GM.

Autonomy/Independence

If your career anchor is autonomy/independence, what you would not give up is the opportunity to define your own work in your own way. If you are in an organization, you want to remain in jobs that allow you flexibility regarding when and how to work. If you cannot tolerate organizational rules and restrictions to any degree, you seek occupations in which you will have the freedom you seek, such as teaching or consulting. You refuse opportunities for promotion or advancement in order to retain autonomy. You may even seek to have a business of your own in order to achieve a sense of autonomy; however, this motive is not the same as the entrepreneurial creativity described later. Your inventory score on this dimension is in the third column of the scoring sheet under the letters AU.

Security/Stability

If your career anchor is security/stability, what you would not give up is employment security or tenure in a job or organization. Your main concern is to achieve a sense of having succeeded so that you can relax. The anchor shows up in concern for financial security (such as pension and retirement plans) or employment security. Such stability may involve trading your loyalty and willingness to do whatever the employer wants from you for some promise of job tenure. You are less concerned with the content of your work and the rank you achieve in the organization, although you may achieve a high level if your talents permit. As with autonomy, everyone has certain needs for security and stability, especially at times when financial burdens may be heavy or when one is facing retirement. People anchored in this way, however, are always concerned with these issues and build their entire self-images around the management of security and stability. Your inventory score on this dimension is in the fourth column of the scoring sheet under the letters SE.

Entrepreneurial Creativity

If your career anchor is entrepreneurial creativity, what you would not give up is the opportunity to create an organization or enterprise of your own, built on your own abilities and your willingness to take risks and to overcome obstacles. You want to prove to the world that you can create an enterprise that is the result of your own effort. You may be working for others in an organization while you are learning and assessing future opportunities, but you will go out on your own as soon as you feel you can manage it. You want your enterprise to be financially successful as proof of your abilities. Your inventory score on this dimension is in the fifth column of the scoring sheet under the letters EC.

Service/Dedication to a Cause

If your career anchor is service/dedication to a cause, what you would not give up is the opportunity to pursue work that achieves something of value, such as making the world a better place to live, solving environmental problems, improving harmony among people, helping others, improving people's safety, curing diseases through new products, and so on. You pursue such opportunities even if it means changing organizations, and you do not accept transfers or promotions that would take you out of work that fulfills your values. Your inventory score on this dimension is in the sixth column of the scoring sheet under the letters SV.

Pure Challenge

If your career anchor is pure challenge, what you would not give up is the opportunity to work on solutions to seemingly unsolvable problems, to win out over tough opponents, or to overcome difficult obstacles. For you, the only meaningful reason for pursuing a job or career is that it permits you to win over the impossible. Some people find such pure challenge in intellectual kinds of work, such as the engineer who is interested only in impossibly difficult designs; some find the challenge in complex, multifaceted situations, such as the strategy consultant who is interested only in clients who are about to go bankrupt and have exhausted all other resources; some find it in interpersonal competition, such as the professional athlete or the salesperson who defines every sale as either a win or a loss. Novelty, variety, and difficulty become ends in themselves; and if something is easy, it becomes immediately boring. Your inventory score on this dimension is in the seventh column of the scoring sheet under the letters CH.

Lifestyle

If your career anchor is lifestyle, what you would not give up is a situation that permits you to balance and integrate your personal needs, your family needs, and the requirements of your career. You want to make all of the major sectors of your life work together toward an integrated whole and you therefore need a career situation that provides enough flexibility to achieve such integration. You may have to sacrifice some aspects of your career (for example, a geographical move that would be a promotion but would upset your total life situation), and you define success in terms broader than just career success. You feel that your identity is more tied up with how you live your total life, where you live, how you deal with your family situation, and how you develop yourself than with any particular job or organization. Your inventory score on this dimension is in the eighth column of the scoring sheet under the letters LS.

Determining Your Own Anchor

You have two sources of information for determining your career anchor: the scores on the orientation inventory and the themes and patterns in the interview. The interview information is the more reliable because it is based on your actual biography, whereas the inventory scores could be biased by your need to see yourself in a certain way.

First rank order the anchor categories from 1 to 8, with 1 being the category that best describes you and 8 being the category that least describes you. This ranking should be done with your interview partner, and the two of you should try to reach consensus based on the interview.

You may find that the ranking became vague in the middle range, but it is important to identify the extremes. As you make the rankings, think in terms of what you could most easily give up (ranks 6, 7, and 8) and what you would have the greatest difficulty in giving up (ranks 3, 2, and 1). Think about the one thing that you would not give up under any circumstance (rank 1). That is your career anchor.

Career Anchor Rankings
Based on Interview

Rank 1 (Career Anchor) _____

Rank 2 _____

Rank 3 _____

Rank 4 _____

Rank 5 _____

Rank 6 _____

Rank 7 _____

Rank 8 _____

Now list your rankings based on your scores on the Career Orientations Inventory (Scoring Sheet on page 10).

Career Anchor Rankings Based on Inventory
Rank 1 (Career Anchor)_____
Rank 2 _____
Rank 3 _____
Rank 4 _____
Rank 5 _____
Rank 6 _____
Rank 7 _____
Rank 8 _____

How close are the two different rankings? If you are off by more than two ranks, do the following:

1. Review the items in the Career Orientations Inventory to see how accurately you believe your answers reflect you;

2. Review your interview answers; and

3. Make your own final decision about where a particular anchor category belongs in the rankings. You also should discuss such discrepancies with your partner and solicit his or her observations.

If the problem is that you believe two or more anchor categories describe you equally well, try to imagine future job situations that would force you to give up one or the other and see what you think you might do. For example, if you feel that you are anchored in both technical/functional competence and general managerial competence, try to imagine what you might do if your organization gave you a choice between running a whole division or being the corporate chief engineer (assuming these jobs to be equivalent in the organizational hierarchy). Most conflicts can be resolved if you think in terms of such future alternatives.

Based on all of the information and a full discussion with your partner, try to make a definitive decision about what your career anchor is and then fill in your final rankings below.

Final Career Anchor Rankings
Rank 1 (Career Anchor) _____
Rank 2 _____
Rank 3 _____
Rank 4 _____
Rank 5 _____
Rank 6 _____
Rank 7 _____
Rank 8 _____

List any unresolved issues below:

6

Practical Implications: What Should You Do Next?

Now that you have analyzed your interview and inventory responses, have rank ordered your anchor categories, and have identified residual issues, how can you best use what you have learned? Several points should be considered:

1. *Learn how to learn more about yourself.* You have learned to be somewhat analytical about your career. Continue to increase your self-insight by finding other opportunities to observe yourself and to draw out the implications of what you observe. Learning about yourself is a lifelong task, because each new experience will reveal new facets. Get in the habit of analyzing your responses to all your new experiences.

2. *Analyze your present job.* How well does your present job fulfill your career needs? Is it congruent with your career anchor? Does it use your talents, meet your needs, and fulfill your values?

3. *Plan ahead.* Does your job need to be redesigned to be more fulfilling in the future? As you contemplate future career moves, are they likely to be congruent with your career anchor? If not, what kinds of adjustments do you need to make to ensure greater congruence? Do you need additional education or training? Do you favor certain kinds of lateral or geographical moves? Are there certain moves to be avoided?

4. *Communicate your needs.* Who needs to know the conclusions that you have reached about yourself in the previous three steps? Are there people in your organization with whom you should share some of your insights and conclusions so that they can do a better job of helping you to plan your career? Do you and members of your family need to discuss these issues to make a better overall life plan?

5. *Become active in managing your career.* None of us has an infinite number of choices when it comes to career management, but all of us have some choices. Determine what your areas of choice are and become active in managing them. As the world becomes more complex, more and more of a burden will fall on each person to manage his or her own career, because it will be more difficult for employers to decide what is best for everyone. Thus, the most important advice is not to become a victim.

If you want to read more about careers, consult the list of resources that follows.

Footnotes

Acknowledgments

[1]Prepared with the support of the Chief of Naval Research, Psychological Sciences Division (Code 452), Organizational Effectiveness Research, Office of Naval Research, Arlington, Virginia 22217, under contract N00014-80-C-0905; NR 170-911.

Chapter 3

[2]The stages outlined here are drawn from the seminal research of Donald Super and are expanded on the basis of the author's own research (Schein, 1978; Super, 1957; Super & Bohn, 1970). Also incorporated is more recent work on career and life stages by Arthur, Hall, & Lawrence (1989); Dalton & Thompson (1986); Derr (1986); Feldman (1988); and Levinson (1978, 1988).

[3]From "The Individual, the Organization, and the Career: A Conceptual Scheme," by E.H. Schein, 1971, *Journal of Applied Behavioral Science, 7,* page 404. Copyright 1971 by JAI Press, Inc. Reprinted by permission.

Further Reading

Arthur, M.B., D.T. Hall and B.S. Lawrence, eds. *Handbook of Career Theory*. New York: Cambridge University Press, 1984.

Arthur, M.B., et al. *Working With Careers: Understanding What We Apply & Applying What We Understand*. New York: Columbia University, 1983.

Bailyn, L., with E.H. Schein. *Living With Technology: Issues at Mid-Career*. Cambridge, MA: MIT Press, 1980.

Dalton, G.W., and P.H. Thompson. *Novations: Strategies for Career Management*. Glenview, IL: Scott, Foresman, 1986.

Derr, C.B. *Managing the New Careerists*. San Francisco: Jossey-Bass, 1986.

Feldman, D.C. *Managing Careers in Organizations*. Glenview, IL: Scott, Foresman, 1988.

Levinson, D.J., et al. *The Seasons of a Man's Life*. New York: Alfred A. Knopf, 1978.

———. *The Seasons of a Woman's Life*. New York, Alfred A. Knopf, 1988.

Schein, E.H. *Career Dynamics: Matching Individual and Organizational Needs*. Reading, MA: Addison-Wesley, 1978.